Table of Contents

The Arctic

Way up north at the top of the world is a remote, frigid wilderness called the Arctic. This vast area touches seven countries and covers eight million square miles (21 million square kilometers) of North America.

The Arctic is bounded on the north by ocean, with an ice pack covering most of the region. Farther inland is the tundra or Arctic prairie. It is snow covered in winter but has a short, glorious summer with spectacular beauty. The third region is the cold desert mountains where little snow falls and vegetation is scarce.

Some of the world's coldest temperatures have been recorded in the Arctic. The thermometer falls below zero for months on end in many areas. In summer, the temperature occasionally hits 80 degrees Fahrenheit (27 degrees Celsius).

The Arctic is the land of the midnight sun. For a few weeks in midsummer, it never becomes dark. The continuous daylight allows more time to prepare for the long, cold winter darkness.

Many Arctic creatures are white in winter and are well covered with fur and feathers. They have short legs, short ears and "snowshoes" on their feet. They produce more than the usual number of offspring. It is a difficult land where every creature must struggle to survive.

America's Arctic

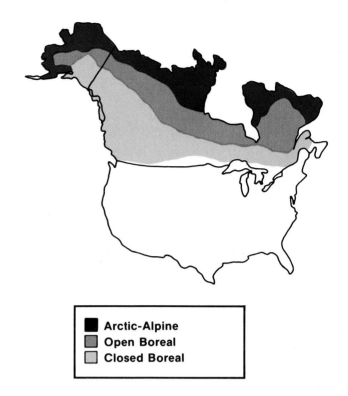

■ Arctic-Alpine
■ Open Boreal
□ Closed Boreal

Icy Shoreline

Ocean

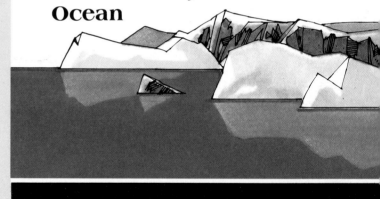

Ptarmigan

This bird blends with the Arctic landscape. In summer it is speckled brown. In winter it is white. The ptarmigan feeds on insects, seeds and berries.

Lemming

The mouse-like lemming is the basic food animal of the Arctic. It lives in tunnels under the snow and in rocks during summer. It digs plants for food.

Musk-Ox

A heavy coat of hair permits the musk-ox to survive on Arctic highlands where snow cover is thin. It uses hooves to uncover sparse grassy plants.

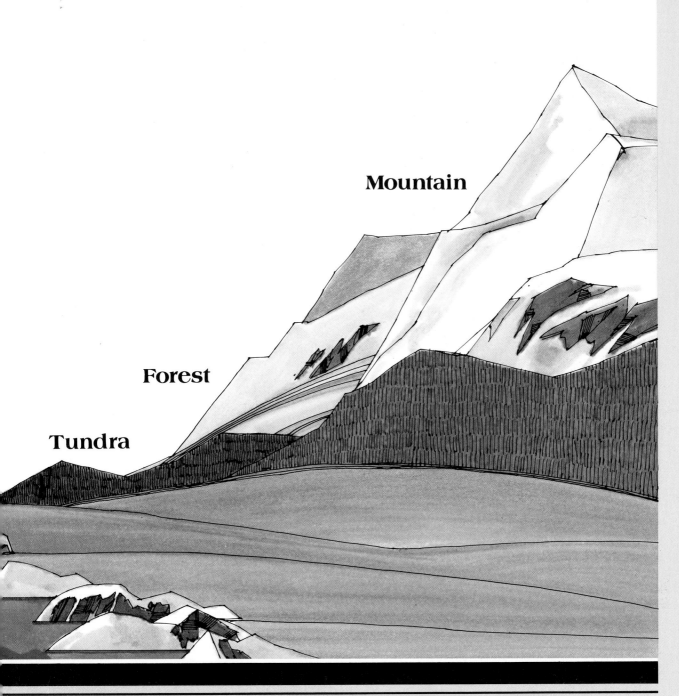

Mountain

Forest

Tundra

Polar Bear

This mighty bear is master of the polar world. It lives near the sea where seals, walrus and dead whales are its food. It also likes mushrooms and berries.

Walrus

Colonies of this big marine mammal live on ice floes and Arctic islands. Big tusks help them gather food from the ocean floor.

Arctic Fox

The snow fox is small with short legs and one of the finest fur coats. Numbers rise and fall with the number of lemmings available for food.

Caribou

Huge herds of caribou wander the tundra, following the same trails year after year. It feeds on lichens, mosses, mushrooms and other plants.

Snowy Owl

This big bird lives in the Arctic year-round. It nests on the ground in tundra country. Lemmings are the favorite food of the snowy owl.

The Ptarmigan

The ptarmigan (the "p" is silent) is a stylish bird with one set of feathers for winter, another for summer. The white winter plumage hides this Arctic grouse in the snow. In spring and summer, when the snow has melted, the ptarmigan's dress changes to shades of gray and brown that blend with the mossy tundra.

The ptarmigan has only a few short weeks to raise a family of chicks. Eggs are laid as bare ground begins to appear through the snow. They must be hatched and chicks well grown before the first cold and snow strike the Arctic in early September. The ample food supply found in the tundra during long summer days helps the young grow rapidly.

In North America there are three kinds of these "eskimo chickens." Willow and rock ptarmigans live their entire lives in the Arctic. White-tailed ptarmigans are at home from the Arctic south into the Rocky and Cascade Mountains of the United States.

The Arctic ptarmigan has many enemies. Foxes, owls and hawks attack it. Eskimos consider it an important part of their food supply. In the United States the white-tailed ptarmigan is prized by hunters, but few are taken because their snowy habitat is hard to reach.

Alaskans named the willow ptarmigan their state bird. It is found nesting in tundra in many locations from beaches to mountains.

Ptarmigan in summer

When the tundra begins to lose its white winter coat and dark mosses appear in patches across the homeland of the ptarmigan, the hens answer the males' courtship calls.

The female scratches a hollow in the ground, often among rocks, where she lays eight to 13 buffy eggs boldly marked with brown. The white-tailed ptarmigan commonly lays fewer eggs than its two relatives.

In choosing a site for her nest, a white-tailed ptarmigan finds a dry location, protected from the wind. It must have an easy escape route in case the hen is threatened while on her nest.

With the female warming the eggs, they hatch in about 22 days. During this time the male is on guard near the nest and warns his mate if danger is near. If the hen is chased from her nest, the male usually attacks the intruder, beating it with his wings.

Leaving the empty shells behind, the chicks soon follow their parents across the tundra in search of buds, leaves and berries to eat.

Ptarmigan in winter

The Arctic summer is short, and ptarmigan parents have time to raise only one family. If the first nest is destroyed, some hens will try again, but chances for success are slim since summer lasts only from late June until September.

During September and October, the ptarmigan begins to put on its winter plumage. The brown feathers of summer are now spotted with white. From November until April the bird is white.

In November when the snow becomes deeper, ptarmigan band together, sometimes in very large flocks. They move to the river valleys, where they feed on buds and twigs.

At the end of the short winter Arctic day, ptarmigan dig holes in the snow where they roost during the long night. New snow may completely bury the sleeping birds by the time morning arrives.

They do not mind the cold as long as they can find food. They can live in temperatures as cold as -50 degrees Fahrenheit (-46 degrees Celsius).

Ptarmigan have sharp claws, and their legs are feathered to their toes. Other members of the grouse family do not have this kind of "snowshoe."

You can see a ptarmigan

You'd have to go to the Arctic tundra to see a willow or a rock ptarmigan. But it is easy to see a white-tailed ptarmigan in the summer, high in Rocky Mountain National Park in Colorado. Trail Ridge Road takes you right to the top of the mountains, where the birds live. They are very tame as they walk slowly ahead of you across the rocky tundra, carpeted with beautiful summer wildflowers.

But be alert! The birds look like their surroundings. If one is standing still or resting on the ground, you may walk right past it and not know it is there.

To see a white-tailed ptarmigan's nest requires a lot of patience and some skill. The sitting females look much like their surroundings, and they refuse to move until almost stepped on. It is not easy to find a ptarmigan's nest. Hens leave their nests to eat only for short periods at dawn and dusk. Only about one in 10 nests is on open tundra. All others are either hidden among rocks or in shrubby thickets.

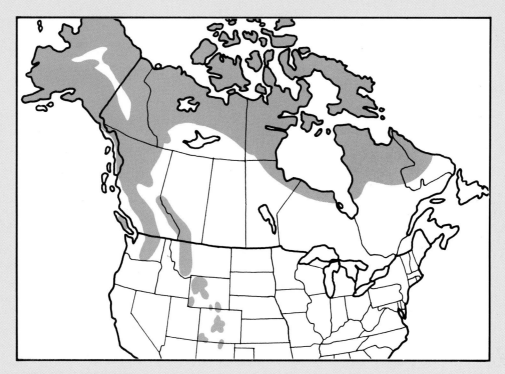

PTARMIGAN FACTS

Habitat: Arctic and high mountain tundra, sheltered valleys in winter.

Habits: Nest on ground. Band together in winter.

Food: Insects, seeds, buds, berries.

Size: Willow, 13-17 inches (33-43 centimeters) long; rock, 11-14 inches (28-36 centimeters); white-tailed, 10-13 inches (25-33 centimeters).

Life Span: Not known; perhaps five years.

Locomotion: Runs rapidly. Flights usually short, alternating fluttering and sailing.

Voice: Cackling notes: clucks, soft hoots. Willow ptarmigan utters deep, raucous calls, "go-out, go-out."

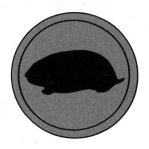

The Lemming

This small rodent plays a major part in the Arctic food chain. Lemmings are the chief food of snowy owls and Arctic foxes; they are also found in the diet of wolves, wolverines, bears, jaegers and skuas. Under certain conditions they become the food of lynxes, weasels, ravens, hawks, even an occasional caribou or, most unlikely, fish.

These mouse-like creatures live close together in the tundra. In summer their nests are among rocks or in tunnels in the ground. Each builds its own runways and tunnels, but they all run about freely on one another's trails. Together, all their trails form a busy network. But they are not friendly and sociable. It is believed they live close together because the habitat is suitable.

In the Arctic area of North America there are several kinds, or species, of lemmings. The most common are the brown lemming and two species of collared lemmings. A lemming has long, soft, silky fur that almost hides its small ears and short tail. Its tail is usually less than an inch (two centimeters) long. Brown lemmings are brown all year. In summer collared lemmings are buffy gray with a darker band along the spine and a tawny band around the throat. In winter they are almost entirely white.

Lemmings do not hibernate

Lemmings find protection from wind and extreme cold by tunneling close to the ground under the snow. Temperatures there seldom get below 20 degrees Fahrenheit (–7 degrees Celsius). In a small hollow under the snow, a lemming builds its nest, a round ball of plant material with an entrance in the side. It sleeps and rests there and occasionally may even give birth to young. It does not have to leave the tunnels to eat; it nibbles the plants exposed by digging. To find more food, a lemming breaks a new path into the snow. These winter pathways are as widespread as the summer network. After the snow has melted, a lacy pattern of ice shows where the snow was trampled by many little feet.

Special kind of foot

Besides the long hair growing on its legs, a lemming has hair on the soles of its feet. This protects and warms its feet and gives it a grip for running

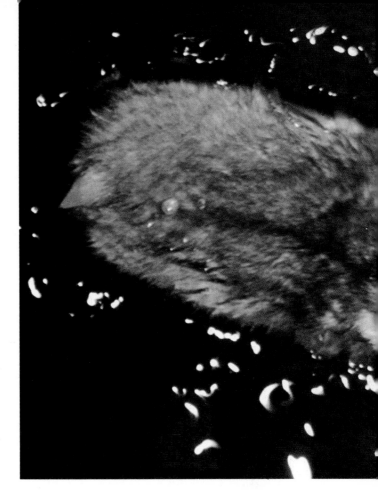

over icy tunnels. In winter the collared lemming develops a horny thickening under the nails of the third and fourth front toes. This added growth is used for digging and is shed in spring.

Plant food for lemmings

Lemmings are vegetarians. They do not eat meat, but feed on sedges, grasses, mosses, lichens, bark, berries, roots and flowers. They sit on their haunches and nibble on pieces held in their front paws. Collared lemmings store grasses, sedges,

weeks old, their eyes are open and they are able to hunt for food with the adults. A lemming can have babies of its own before it is fully grown. There are usually two to six young in a litter, but there may be as many as 11. A female lemming may have two or more litters each year. The short time needed to grow up, the large litter size and the number of litters per year can lead to rapid population increases. This happens when weather and food conditions are favorable. When lemmings are plentiful, Arctic foxes and snowy owls are also plentiful.

willow catkins and moss underground. Their food and their nests are made up of the same kinds of plants.

More and more lemmings

Most lemmings are born between April and September, though some litters are born during the winter. There are 19 to 22 days between mating and the birth of the young. Both parents care for the offspring. By the time the babies are two

The strange travels of lemmings

European lemmings are famous for what seem to be mass suicidal journeys. We now know that North American lemmings also make such journeys, although perhaps less often. These are not true migrations, for migration helps an animal stay alive. The lemmings' travels generally result in death.

The pressures of being con-

17

fined in close quarters under the snow begin to affect the animals' behavior. When warmer weather arrives, they welcome the chance to leave their tunnels. A mass movement will begin with perhaps one lemming feeling nervous and quarrelsome. In time others become irritable. In the excitement of being out in the sun and open air, a lemming sets off as if on a purposeful search. A few follow it, then more, and eventually, a whole mass is on the move. In a kind of madness, they run straight in whatever direction they have started. They pass right over or through obstacles. If they come to a river or the sea, they swim. Hordes of lemmings are followed and attacked by many mammals and birds. In rivers and lakes, or the sea, they are even eaten by fish. Most of those that escape predators eventually drown in the sea from exhaustion.

Many forces bring about this strange behavior in lemmings. Perhaps if we learn more about them we will better understand how crowded conditions in cities affect human beings and their behavior.

Population ups and downs

The increases in populations that seem to trigger these mass journeys tend to develop in cycles of four years. Some scientists think the highs and lows are due to the lemmings' ability to reproduce rapidly when food is abundant. At a certain point, their numbers are so huge that they overgraze the food supply. Starvation follows, and the population pendulum swings back to low.

Another theory is that overcrowding causes changes in the way the organs of the body

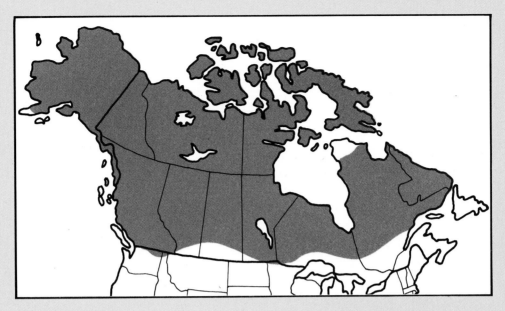

LEMMING FACTS

Habitat: Arctic tundra.

Habits: Active night or day, winter or summer. Builds runways and tunnels in earth and snow. Has four year cycles of abundance.

Food: Grass, sedges, mosses, lichens, bark, berries, fruits, roots and flowers.

Size and Weight: Collared lemmings: Length, 4¾-5½ inches (12-14 centimeters); tail 2-16 inches (5-40 centimeters); weight 1³/₅-2²/₅ ounces (45-68 grams). Brown lemmings: Length, 4½-5½ inches (11-14 centimeters); tail ⁴/₅-1¹/₆ inches (two-three centimeters); weight, 2½-4 ounces (71-113 grams).

Lifespan: In captivity, over two years.

Locomotion: Scurries through tunnels and runways.

Voice: Squeals and chuckling sounds; also chattering of teeth.

work. This brings about death or a reduction in the number of young produced. As the population declines, the pressure of overcrowding eases. The lemmings' bodies return to normal, and the populations begin to grow again.

Indirectly, the population of these small animals is important to the Eskimos. Because lemmings are a major food for foxes, during years when lemmings are abundant there will be more foxes—and more furs for trappers.

The Musk-Ox

The musk-ox is a strange-looking, shaggy beast with a humped back. Eskimos call it *oomingmak*, or "the bearded one." It is armed with curved horns, and has a very bad temper. Musk-oxen do not like to share their territory with any other creatures. A minor noise or movement will make the males snort. They also lower and wag their heads from side to side. The animal looks like a cross among a cow, sheep and bison. However, it is related to none of these.

A leftover from the Ice Age, musk-oxen once lived with the mighty mammoths, woolly rhinoceroses and beavers the size of bears. A million years ago, when vast glaciers lowered the oceans, the musk-oxen crossed to North America on a land bridge that joined Asia and Alaska. The animals moved as far south as Iowa and New York. When the Ice Age came to an end, only a few musk-oxen survived in the high Arctic of Greenland. Eventually, the population recovered and spread to northern Canada and Alaska.

The first whites to enter the Arctic found a great many musk-oxen. They also found that the animals provided meat and warm robes. Between 1850 and 1920, thousands were slaughtered. If musk-oxen did not live in such remote areas, they might have been totally destroyed.

Today, the musk-ox is protected and doing better. More than 1,500 live in mainland Canada, about 5,000 on the Canadian Arctic islands and perhaps that many more in Greenland. They have been introduced into Norway and Spitsbergen and were reestablished in Alaska in 1931. The most recent transplant was into the Soviet Union.

Fearless, savage survivor

Musk-oxen can be dangerous. When attacked, the herd gathers into a tight circle, heads and horns pointing out. Hidden inside the furry circle, calves are protected. The adults make lightning-quick charges out from the circle, trying to gore the enemy. This defense usually works against wolves and polar bears, but not against humans with guns and spears.

The musk from which these creatures get their name is stored in two glands, one just under each eye. When attacked, they rub the gland on their legs and release an odor that discourages their enemies.

Above all else, musk-oxen are built to survive the severe cold. They look heavier than their 600 to 800 pounds (270 to 360 kilograms) because they have two coats. The bulky outer coat covers a thick inner layer of wool. The hair on the back is five to six inches (13 to 15 centimeters) long. At the neck, chest and rump, it .is two to three feet (60 to 90 centimeters) long. It hangs, like a shirt, straight from the animal's belly and sides almost to the ground. Sometimes this hair freezes to the ground and the animal can't move. If it gets stuck, it will starve to death.

Special ice hooves

Like many hooved animals, the musk-ox's black hooves are especially equipped for its environment. They have sharp edges that spread when weight is put on them. These edges cut into the ice and allow the animal to walk up or down icy hills.

Golden fleece of the arctic

Some musk-oxen live in captivity. Because the meat tastes like good beef, musk-oxen are raised as a kind of northland cattle. Leather from the hides is of good quality. The musk-ox's greatest attraction, however, is its super wool, called *qiviut*. This golden fleece of the Arctic does not shrink and will take any dye. One pound (454 grams) of this wool can be spun into a 40 strand thread 25 miles (40 kilometers) long!

Battles to the death

Bull, or male, musk-oxen are especially touchy as the Arctic summer draws to an end. It is the time when they will seek cows, or females, to make up their herds.

Battles for cows can be to the death. When two bulls come together in combat, they ram each other time and time again. When they hit, they often go straight up in the air. These battles last for hours and may end only when one meets its death on the horns or under the hooves of the winner.

When the fight is over, the victor mates with the cow for which he has fought. By late September, just as early winter arrives, the battles end for another year.

Calf's first crucial hour

Musk-oxen are born in April or May, when storms are common and the temperature can be 30 degrees Fahrenheit (-34 degrees Celsius) below zero. Imagine the shock of birth—a calf drops from its mother's warm body into a world that is suddenly 130 degrees (70 degrees Celsius) colder. Wrapped in dark, dense curly wool, the calf's steaming body is licked dry by the mother. In a few minutes the 20 pound (nine kilogram) calf staggers to its feet and starts to suck rich milk. Within a week it adds Arctic grasses to its diet.

Most musk-ox calves survive birth. They remain with their mothers for at least a year. Musk-ox cows give birth only every other year.

During its first summer, the calf's only real worry is hordes of mosquitoes and blackflies. Fortunately, its thick coat helps protect it against these pests.

The calf's main business is eating. By late summer, it feeds on almost anything that grows: sedges, grasses, blueberries and sprouts of small trees. Like

MUSK-OXEN FACTS

Habitat: The "high Arctic," on the extreme northern fringe of tundra bordering the polar seas. The cold desert has little snow, leaving the ground bare except for the low-growing plants on which the musk-oxen feed.

Habits: A grazing herd, numbering from three to more than 100. Has a bad temper. In winter it finds slopes and ridges protected from the icy wind. Winter and summer ranges are only a few miles (kilometers) apart.

Food: Grazes on sedges, grasses, herbs, mosses and willow.

Size and Weight: Five feet (1.5 meters) high and seven feet (2.1 meters) long; 600-800 pounds (270-360 kilograms); 20 pounds (nine kilograms) at birth.

Life Span: Believed to be at least 23 years.

Locomotion: Swims well; runs well, but not very fast.

Voice: Usually silent, but when excited, gives various snorts and grunts.

cattle, the musk-ox has no upper front teeth and must pull food free by tightly grabbing it between its leathery tongue or lower teeth and the roof of its mouth.

The calf's life is a pleasant one as it frolics around the herd, perhaps with another calf or two. But within six months it will be fighting a life and death battle against winter.

The Polar Bear

"Ruler of the North" is a perfect title for the mighty polar bear. Its empire is the frozen wasteland at the top of the world. Like a powerful ruler, this enormous beast is feared by nearly every creature in the Arctic.

A polar bear begins life in a snug den beneath winter snow. A newborn cub is only about the size of a guinea pig and is blind and helpless. The mother bear's warmth and rich milk helps the cub grow rapidly. By spring it is a husky 25 to 30 pounds (11 to 14 kilograms).

Polar bears are always on the move, migrating hundreds of miles each year. It is not unusual for a bear to travel 75 miles (120 kilometers) a day in search of food. Sometimes polar bears catch rides on floating islands of ice called floes. They also are excellent swimmers, almost as comfortable in the water as they are on land. At other times, they shuffle along the shoreline in search of food.

Polar bears are found in the polar regions of Norway, Greenland, Canada, the Soviet Union and the United States. No one really knows how many of the rare white bears are left in the world; perhaps there are 10,000. Each bear roams about 270 square miles (700 square kilometers) of territory. To keep them from becoming even more scarce, the Arctic nations are working to protect and manage these magnificent creatures and preserve their habitat.

White on white

Polar bears are well equipped to live comfortably in their icy empire. Their white coat makes it difficult for them to be seen on the snow and ice. Long guard hairs in their dense fur trap a layer of air, giving the animal extra warmth. The inner layer of fur is so thick that water cannot get to the skin when the bears are swimming. Oil in their hair and skin also helps to "waterproof" the bears.

Polar bears are the only bears that have hair on the bottoms of their feet. It provides warmth and keeps them from slipping on ice and snow.

If we lived in a world of bright white, as the polar bear does, we would have to wear sunglasses all the time to protect our eyes. The polar bear has natural "shades"—a thin, inner eyelid that the bear can lower to keep the brightness from hurting.

Marathon swimmer

Polar bears spend so much time in the water that some scientists call them marine mammals. When swimming, they paddle with their partly webbed front paws. The hind legs stay almost motionless in the water and are used as rudders. The air spaces in their fur and a heavy layer of body fat help polar bears float. They can lie on the surface of the water for a long time without paddling.

When cubs get tired of swimming, they hang onto their mother's tail with their teeth, and she tows them along. Sometimes they ride on her back.

Polar bears have been seen swimming more than a hundred miles (160 kilometers) from the nearest land. They swim with little effort and can probably cover more than 200 miles (300 kilometers) at a stretch without stopping to rest.

A life alone

Polar bears are usually found alone. Two exceptions are mothers with cubs and adults during the breeding season.

A few days after mating, the male, or boar, and the she-bear, called a sow, part and probably never meet again. In the middle of winter, when the sow is in her den, she gives birth to cubs.

There is another time when polar bears come together. That is when a whale, walrus or large seal has died and washed ashore. A whale or an 800 pound (360 kilogram) bearded seal makes a generous meal for every polar bear within smelling distance—

up to 20 miles (30 kilometers) away. The rotting meat of a dead animal is called carrion, and polar bears never pass up a chance to have carrion for dinner. Their favorite food, however, is seal.

Super seal hunter

Fur on the bottom of their paws not only keeps polar bears' feet warm, but also allows them to approach seals silently. Some- times the bears get close to a seal and then pounce on it, as a cat would. More often, they lie stock still for hours next to a hole in the ice. Seals must come to the surface of the water to breathe about every eight minutes. When one pops up in a hole, the bear's huge paw flashes out and flips the seal onto the ice, killing it instantly. The bear blends with its white surroundings and is not easily seen. It often hides its black nose with its right paw while hunting. Polar bears usually seem to use

their left paw to make the kill.

The bear stuffs itself with seal blubber, the rich layer of fat under the animal's skin. The bear eats flesh only in hard times, when hunting is very poor. After feasting on the blubber, the polar bear often leaves the rest of the seal carcass for the Arctic foxes. Foxes sometimes follow polar bears, knowing that they will provide an easy dinner.

With its belly full, the bear might frolic about like a cub. It turns somersaults, prances across the ice and slides down icy slopes on its rump.

An icy nursery

Boars and sows without cubs are active most of the winter. They may stay out even when the temperature drops to -65 degrees Fahrenheit (-54 Celsius). But if the polar bears want to escape extremely harsh weather, they find shelter in a cave or under an ice ledge. Here they sleep until the weather improves.

Some polar bears, usually females with first-year cubs, spend part of the winter sleeping in dens. Females who are expecting young dig maternity dens in October or November. They stay there with their babies until late March or early April.

Using her front paws, the sow digs an entrance way, carefully carving and packing the walls. An average den is seven feet (two meters) long, five feet (1.5 meters) wide and three feet (one meter) high, with one or more rooms. When the sow goes inside for her winter sleep, she blocks the entrance with snow and opens a three inch (eight centimeter) wide hole in the roof of her sleeping room for air.

A mighty bear grows from a tiny baby

Snug inside her den beneath the snow, the sow is in her winter sleep. Her metabolism, or the rate at which her body uses energy, is much slower than normal. She sleeps very deeply, but not as deeply as a true hibernator—an animal that spends the whole winter in a deathlike trance.

In December or January, the sow awakens. It is time for her cubs to be born. Young polar bear mothers sometimes have only one cub, but usually there are two. The sow licks them dry and cuddles the tiny babies so they can nurse. The newborn cubs are about the size of guinea pigs, and each weighs about one pound (454 grams). Its mother weighs 700 times that much! For the first six weeks of their lives, the cubs' eyes and ears are sealed shut. They have almost no fur, and the mother is careful to keep them snuggled close. Although the den is 40 degrees Fahrenheit (23 degrees Celsius) warmer than the temperature outside, it is still below freezing. The cubs would die if they strayed from their mother's warm body.

The mother bear sleeps for

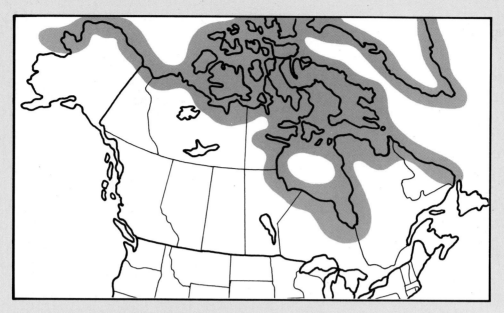

POLAR BEAR FACTS

Habitat: Arctic land areas, polar seas and ice floes.

Habits: Solitary, wanders over great distances.

Food: Favorite is seal. Also eats lemmings, salmon and other fish, carrion and, occasionally, a young walrus. Sometimes eats mushrooms, grasses and berries.

Size and Weight: Adult male is eight-nine feet (two-three meters) from nose to tail and weighs 800-1,000 pounds (363-454 kilograms). Adult female is about six feet (two meters) long and weighs about 700 pounds (320 kilograms).

Life Span: Probably 25-30 years.

Locomotion: Shuffling walk. Can run as fast as 25 miles (40 kilometers) per hour when chased. Powerful swimmer.

Voice: Rarely makes sounds. Cubs hum, whimper and whine, sometimes screech. Adults roar.

most of the rest of the winter, waking a few times each day to nurse her cubs. Her milk is very rich, and the youngsters grow quickly.

When the cubs come out of the den in spring, they each weigh 25 to 30 pounds (11 to 14 kilograms), are nearly 30 inches (80 centimeters) long, and have woolly coats.

Polar bear cubs stay with their mother for one and a half to two years. During this time, she teaches them the lessons of survival in the wilderness.

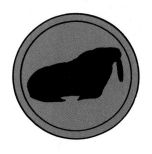

The Walrus

What animal is 11 feet (three meters) long, weighs 2,000 pounds (900 kilograms)—as much as 12 or more men— has thick, wrinkled skin and great ivory tusks? You might answer, "It's an elephant." But in addition, this animal has fins instead of feet, seems to have no ears and lives in the Arctic. It is a walrus, or as the Norwegians call it, *hvalros*—whale-horse.

The walrus is a marine mammal—that is, it lives in the sea. Like other mammals, its babies suck milk from their mother. It has short, sparse, grayish-brown hair. On its face, bristly hairs, coarser than porcupine quills, grow in neat rows. While it can swim well, it must come to the surface to breathe air.

The walrus is also a pinniped mammal—it has fins or flippers instead of feet. Its hind flippers can be turned forward and fanned out so that they can be used to push, as the walrus lumbers over the ice. Some of its pinniped relatives cannot do this and move on land only by wriggling their bodies.

The walrus is graceful and powerful in water. Its fins have five long "fingers" connected by webs of skin. When they are spread, the webs provide a broad paddle that gives added power for swimming. Although the walrus is a strong swimmer, it cannot spend all of its time in water. When it is tired it must find an island or ice floe to rest on or it will die.

A sociable animal

For the most part, walruses live in colonies of a few to more than a hundred bulls, cows and calves. In groups, they travel back and forth between wintering areas in the Bering Sea and Hudson Bay and their breeding grounds in the Arctic Ocean. On these travels, a small calf clings with its flippers to the back of its mother's neck as she swims and dives. Walruses lie together on beaches and ice floes when courting, mating and giving birth to young. Even the old males, past breeding age, will bask together on a sunny beach.

A different kind of family life

When walruses arrive at their breeding grounds in spring, each bull mates with several females. A bull defends a certain territory during this season. He may be so busy patrolling that he goes without food for as long as two months.

But he does not guard a harem of cows. The cows move freely from one territory to another territory.

After she is four or five years old, a cow bears one calf every other year, sometimes every third year. It is almost a

year between the time of mating and the birth of the calf. The newborn baby is about four feet (1.2 meters) long, weighs 120 to 130 pounds (55 to 60 kilograms) —about as much as a grown woman—and can swim almost immediately.

However, because it has no tusks, a young walrus must depend on its mother for food until it is nearly two years old. By then its tusks will have developed, and it can get food for itself. In the meantime, its food is its mother's milk, which is especially rich. Walruses are devoted parents, and the mother can be depended on to protect her youngster from danger.

Built for the world of water

Ages ago when the walrus's ancestors were still land animals, their flipper feet must have been ordinary legs. Today, these limbs are built for water.

The four narrow slits through which the walrus breathes and hears can be tightly closed when it is under water. It can make itself sleek and streamlined for swimming.

The walrus swims head down and uses its long ivory tusks as a rake or pick to grub food from the ocean bottom. The bristles on its muzzle help move the food into its mouth. Walruses prefer clams and other mollusks and small sea life. They will dive as deep as 300 feet (90 meters) although they prefer fishing in shallower places.

It was once thought that the walrus cracked shells with its back teeth, then spit out the shells. But it may be that the walrus sucks the meat out of the shells. The tusks are fierce weapons in battles with other bulls and against enemies such as sharks or polar bears. Sometimes they are used as hooks to help a walrus scoot along on the

ground or ice or to climb from the water onto a slippery ice floe.

Tusks are really overgrown teeth. By the time a walrus is two years old, its tusks are three

to four inches (8 to 10 centimeters) long. An adult male may have tusks two to three feet (60 to 90 centimeters) long, but the females' tusks are shorter.

Blubber, a very useful fat

Under the leathery skin of an adult walrus is a six inch (15 centimeter) thick layer of fat called blubber. This keeps the body warm in the icy waters and chilly air of the North. Although the water or air temperature may be around freezing, the body beneath the blubber remains at about 100 degrees Fahrenheit (37 degrees Celsius). Blubber is oily, lighter in weight than water and helps the animal to float. It supplies energy when bulls go without food while defending their territory. It also helps a cow produce milk for her calf.

Buffalo of the arctic

For centuries Eskimos have used various parts of the walrus in many ways. The skin is stretched over a frame to make a boat, and strips of skin are used as cord. The meat is food for both humans and dogs. Oil from the blubber is burned for light; walrus intestines can be used for making windows. Crafts-workers carve beautiful art pieces from the ivory. Realizing the importance of this animal to their lives, the natives of the North used to regulate the number taken each year.

However, in recent years people have not been so careful about preserving this species. Rifles have made hunting and killing much easier. Commercial demands for meat, oil and ivory are great. Progress is being made on solving problems of protection and control. Walrus populations seem to be holding up. However, only continued awareness, planning and enforcement will assure the future of this great beast.

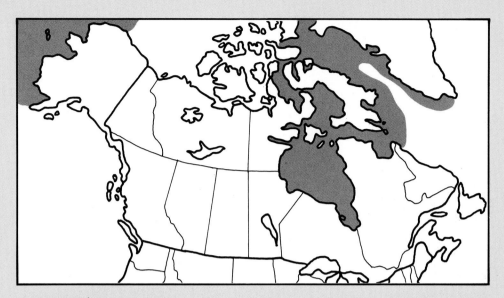

WALRUS FACTS

Habitat: Water, ice floes and islands of the Arctic.

Habits: Bulls mate with more than one cow. Mates bear young and rest on land; get food from the sea.

Food: Mollusks and other small marine life. Largest walruses reported to eat seals.

Size and Weight: Adult bull, 10-12 feet (3-3.6 meters) long, five feet (1.5 meters) high, about 2,700 pounds (1,225 kilograms); female, nine feet (three meters) long, 1,800 pounds (816 kilograms).

Lifespan: Twenty to 25 years.

Locomotion: Swims; lumbers along on land with its four webbed feet, sometimes helped by pulling with its tusks.

Voice: Bellows like the voice of a St. Bernard dog; trumpeting similar to that of elephant.

The Arctic Fox

No land is too difficult for the rascally Arctic fox. It thrives in the fierce Arctic winters, climbs the steepest rock piles and travels without fear across dangerous ice floes. The fox ranges all across the Arctic tundra of North America, Eurasia and the islands of the northern seas.

The Arctic fox population increases very rapidly when there is a good supply of food. There may be as many as 14 kits in one family and the average is 10. They grow to maturity and learn how to find food for themselves in the short Arctic summer. By September the Arctic fox young are on their own.

The dense winter fur of the Arctic foxes appears in two colors, pure white and blue. In the more common pure white, only the eyes, nose, claws and a few hairs in the tail are black. In the blue coat, the fox looks smoky blue or gray. Both coats turn brownish-gray in the summer.

The Arctic fox has little or no fear, even of humans. This curious animal will approach humans quite closely and bark at them like a domestic dog. It will carry tools from construction sites and oil wells a mile (1.6 kilometers) or more from the sites. One British botanist turned away from his wash basin for a moment and then looked back just in time to see a fox trotting away with his bar of soap! The fox's craftiness helps it survive.

Survival is a way of life

Mass starvation, wolves, hordes of mosquitoes, terrible winter weather and Eskimo trappers are all enemies of the Arctic fox. But this amazing animal survives. Here are some of the ways:

Like its neighbors, the varying hare and the polar bear, the fox has a dense covering of hair on the soles of its feet. The hair keeps the feet warm and works like snowshoes to make travel easier in deep snow.

The Arctic fox is smaller than any of its warm-land cousins. Its short ears, short legs and compact body hold in heat, with the help of long dense fur—all a part of its cold weather machinery.

Lemmings are the fox's chief source of food. Because the number of lemmings goes through highs and lows about every four years, the fox populations also change at about the same rates. Faced with starvation, the fox will migrate south, much like the snowy owl, in search of food. At other times the fox will follow the polar bear, eating leftovers of its kills.

In summer, foxes will sometimes gorge on sea birds, their eggs and their young. When this kind of food is in good supply, the Arctic fox will store the surplus in holes and under rocks. One stockpile contained 65 sea birds, another 103, and still another contained 107. The Arctic is the only member of the fox family that stores food to prepare for the winter.

A hard world for kits

In February, when icy winds still howl and the snow piles high, Arctic foxes start to raise a family. Young, unmated males fight for females. When the growling and biting ends, the winner trots off with his mate to find a den. The pair will either dig a new den or rebuild an old one. Some dens may be used for centuries.

Kits are born 52 days after the pair have mated. If there is much food available, as many as 14 kits may be born in one litter. The average of 10 is twice as many as red or gray foxes produce. Each kit weighs about two ounces (55 grams) and is covered with short, fuzzy brown hair. When its eyes open 10 days later, it starts to walk. Because the summers are so short, kits leave the den when they are only a month old. By July, they are following their parents around the tundra. They learn to hunt and take care of themselves quickly. By September, the young are on their own. They must leave the territory of their parents because there is not enough food for a whole family. If food is scarce, young foxes have no stockpiles and move south. Few return.

The eskimo and the fox

For the Eskimo, the Arctic fox means money. The snow-white pelts bring trappers $30 or more. Blue pelts are even more valuable. A good trapper may catch several hundred foxes a winter. In Canada alone, 10,000 to 80,000 fox pelts are

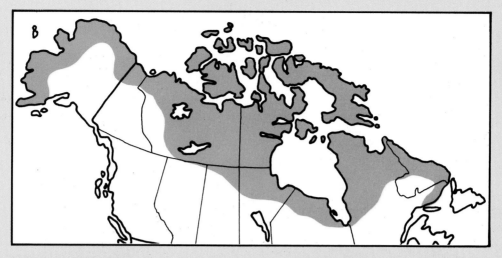

ARCTIC FOX FACTS

Habitat: Barren Arctic tundra, coastal regions and ice floes.

Habits: Active nearly any hour (the sun doesn't set in the Arctic summer). Curious and shows little fear of people. Travels alone. When food is scarce, will migrate south.

Food: Mostly lemmings, but in the summer will gorge on sea birds. Also eats mice, voles, sea urchins, mollusks and crustaceans. Will eat remains of polar bear kills and dead whales. The only fox that stores food.

Size and Weight: Small among foxes, average 7-15 pounds (three-seven kilograms), record of 21 pounds (10 kilograms); 9-12 inches (23-30 centimeters) high and about 30 inches (76 centimeters) total length.

Life Span: In captivity, about 14 years, but in the wild most have trouble surviving first year.

Locomotion: Because of short legs, top speed is 20-25 miles (30-40 kilometers) per hour; travels more than any other member of the dog family in North America.

Voice: Mostly barks, but also whines, yelps and growls.

sold each year. The profits buy snowmobiles, radios, tools, guns, clothes and traps to catch more foxes.

The Arctic fox is easy to catch. Its fearlessness and curiosity about humans make it an easy victim. One popular bait used in fox traps is toothpaste!

The Arctic fox is still the most hunted and trapped animal of the Arctic, but it is not endangered. As long as people wear furs, fox pelts will be valued throughout the world for their beauty and warmth.

The Caribou

If you were to fly over the summer tundra of Canada and Alaska, you might see long streams of dark brown marks on the ground. Some hillsides might look as though they were splitting open at the seams, with dark soil spilling out. Those endless streams of brown are caribou trails that have been carved for thousands of years by the animals' hooves. In some places they are more than two feet (60 centimeters) deep.

Barren ground caribou are constantly on the move, stopping just long enough to feed and rest. In the spring, the huge herds leave the forests where they have spent the winter. They migrate northward to calving grounds in high, rocky hills. Here, cows give birth to their young. In summer or early fall, the herds move down to the lush tundra, called the Arctic prairie. In late autumn, triggered by the first heavy snowfall, the caribou again work their way south to the jackpine and spruce forests where they will spend the winter.

The search for food is probably the main reason that caribou must always be moving. Weather conditions, wolves, and insects and pests may also keep them on the go.

Specially outfitted by nature

For us, –60 degrees Fahrenheit (–50 degrees Celsius) temperature would be unbearable. For caribou, cold is no problem. A caribou's winter coat combines long, stiff, air-filled guard hairs and short, fine, curly underfur. It's almost like wearing one fur coat on top of another, with a layer of warm air between.

Caribou feet are unusually large for the size of the animals. In winter, the sharp, horny hooves serve as "snowshoes." The caribou is sure-footed on hard snow and ice.

Caribou can smell the tasty plants that grow under the snow in winter. The animals chop and paw at the snow with the sharp edges of their front hooves, throwing showers of white behind them. They can scrape through as much as two feet (60 centimeters) of snow to expose plants.

The pads in the center of the caribou's hooves, which are covered with short hair in the winter, change for the summer. The hard rim of the hooves wears away to expose a larger area of spongy pad for better walking on boggy tundra.

Growing up fast

The first caribou to begin the spring migration are the cows that are ready to give birth. They often travel more than 500 miles (800 kilometers) to arrive at the calving ground in late May. There, surrounded by melting snowdrifts, cows give birth during the first two weeks of June. If the calves are born too early and are exposed to a blizzard or too much cold wind, they may die. In some years, as many as half of all newborn caribou calves die during their first month.

Though they have a hard life, baby caribou develop quickly. They can stand within an hour of birth and can run two hours later. At the ripe old age of just one day, they can outrun a human. In less than three days, they keep up with the herd.

Weighing 10 to 13 pounds (four to six kilograms) at birth, the calves double their weight in two weeks. They nurse at first, then begin to graze when they are two to three weeks old. At four weeks, they begin to sprout their first stubby set of antlers. By August, they no longer depend upon mothers.

Crowning glory

Caribou are the only members of the deer family in which both sexes grow antlers. Bulls, or males, sometimes have antlers more than 5½ feet (1.7 meters) high that measure four feet (1.2 meters) from one branch to the other. Although impressive, the females' antlers aren't so magnificent.

Caribou antlers are unique. They are neither cleanly pronged, like the antlers of a white-tailed deer, nor heavily webbed, like those of a moose. They are called semi-palmated, which means partially webbed. Two tall beams branch upward and backward, each having many smaller branches and points. In front of these grow shorter, webbed antlers. In addition, a broad antler, called a "shovel," grows forward over the eyes. Caribou sometimes grow two shovels.

Each spring new antlers grow from the caribou's skull. By summer, they are covered with "velvet," a kind of skin that nourishes the soft antlers with blood. They reach their glorious

maximum growth by September. The antlers get hard, and the velvet begins to dry up. As the bulls travel, they scrape off the velvet and polish their antlers by rubbing them against willows and small spruces.

The caribou's breeding season, which in the deer family is called the rut, is in November. This is when the bulls put their antlers to use, challenging other bulls for the right to breed cows. Heads lowered, chins tucked between their front feet, two bulls face each other. Charging, they crash their antlers together. After that, the battle turns into a pushing contest. Each bull tries to overcome his opponent, watching for a chance to slash the other with his sharp antlers.

By December or January, the breeding season is over, and the bulls' antlers fall off. The cows don't drop theirs until spring. Soon after that, both sexes start to grow a new set.

When trotting, the caribou carries its head stiffly in front of its body, with the massive antlers lying along its back. Holding them in this way keeps them from swaying, throwing the caribou off balance.

Eskimo staff of life

The caribou has been as important to the north country Indians and the Eskimos as the bison was to the Plains Indians. Every part of the caribou is used for food, clothing or tools.

Fat fuels lamps and is eaten or used for cooking. Sometimes it is whipped and bits of cooked caribou meat are added. This strange-sounding dish is the Eskimo's version of ice cream.

Caribou hides are prized for their exceptional warmth. The skins are used for winter pants, gloves, socks and parkas. The heavy hides from bulls make good sleeping mats or pads for sleds. Thin pieces of leg skin are used for boots.

In some areas, Eskimos have no other food source and may starve when they cannot obtain caribou.

Caribou cousins

There is more than one kind of caribou. The barren ground caribou is the most familiar because of its amazing migration habits. The woodland caribou, largest of the North American caribou, migrates only short distances. Usually, it travels no farther than up and down a mountain.

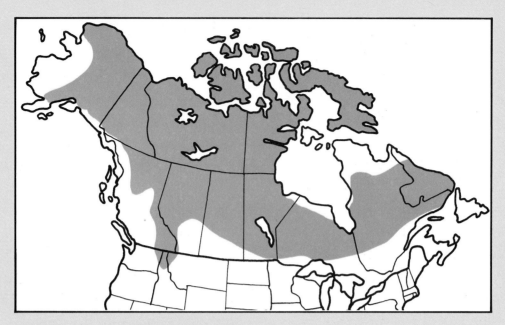

BARREN GROUND CARIBOU FACTS

Habitat: Winter: spruce and jackpine forest. Summer: Arctic tundra.

Habits: Among the most migratory of all mammals. Prefers to feed in daylight.

Food: In winter, lichens, often called reindeer moss. Also sedges, dwarf willow, blueberry, bearberry, horsetail, cranberry, Labrador tea and many types of mushrooms.

Size and Weight: Three and one half to four feet (1-1.2 meters) at shoulder. Bulls weigh 250-400 pounds (113-180 kilograms); cows are between 150-250 pounds (68-113 kilograms).

Life Span: Can live 10-13 years, but average is probably less than five.

Locomotion: Walks and trots. When panicked, will gallop at speeds of 30 miles (50 kilometers) per hour for short distances.

Voice: Practically none. Most communication is through body movements. Cows and calves communicate with low, coughing grunts.

The Greenland caribou is the same species that is found in northern Eurasia. There it is called the reindeer and has been tamed and herded for centuries. The North American caribou doesn't do well in captivity, but reindeer seem to enjoy receiving human protection and handling.

The Snowy Owl

Y ou may have to wait for an "owl year" before you see a snowy owl in the United States. This big, white, ghostlike bird usually is content to remain year-round in its homeland in the open tundra country of the North. Despite severe cold and the harsh country, it can survive. It has a thick covering of soft, fluffy feathers to protect it from cold and storms. The bird is an excellent hunter.

The snowy is among our largest owls. It is 20 to 27 inches (51 to 69 centimeters) long and its wings spread 50 to 60 inches (130 to 150 centimeters). Females are slightly larger than their mates. Both have hairy white feathers covering their legs and toes, often hiding their long curved claws. The snowy owl, however, is not all white. Males are closer to pure white than the females, though they also have some dark markings on their backs and tails.

These owls are often quite fierce in defending their nests, and there are reports of attacks on humans who came too close. As with most other birds of prey, however, there is a great difference among individuals. While some may attack or try to frighten a human, others are shy and will fly away.

The flight of the snowy owl is much like that of the great horned owl—silent, powerful and direct. But the white owl is not likely to be mistaken for any other bird.

An owl's year

Snowy owls depend largely on lemmings, small Arctic rodents, and hares for food. These animals increase greatly in numbers when tundra conditions are good. In turn, the owls do well as their food supply increases. But every so often there is a sudden drop in the number of lemmings and hares. When this happens the snowy owls and other wildlife that depend upon them for food are in trouble.

Facing starvation and death, great numbers of snowy owls leave their barren tundra home and fly south in search of other food. Such a time is called an "owl year," and you may find these big white birds as far south as the Carolinas, Dakotas, Illinois and West Virginia. In one owl year, 1926-27, an observer kept records of 2,368 different reports of snowy owls seen in the United States. There must have been thousands more not seen or not reported. Some years there are almost no reports of snowy owls in southern areas.

Home life of the snowy

Nests of the snowy owl are found on the tundra, north of where trees grow. They have been found as far north as there is land not covered with ice and snow in summer. The owls prefer to nest in places where there are low rocky ridges and small mounds. These elevated places serve as nesting sites and for lookout points from which the males hunt and watch for enemies.

The Arctic summer is short, and the owls nest early, often while there is still snow on the ground. There must be time after hatching for young owlets to learn to hunt food and to prepare for the long winter.

Life in the arctic

Most owls are night hunters, but because of the long Arctic summer days, the snowy owl is a daytime hunter.

To catch its prey, especially lemmings, the owl often stands motionless on a ridge or mound and waits for the rodents to come near. With lightning speed, the big bird seizes its prey in its long, sharp talons, or claws.

Following an "owl year" when lemmings and hares are scarce on the tundra, few owls will nest at all. Those that do must hunt constantly to find enough of the scarce food to keep their young alive.

SNOWY OWL FACTS

Habitat: North of trees on open tundra country to the shores of the Arctic Sea.

Habits: Non-migratory except in winters when food supply fails. Invade United States in search of food in so-called "owl years." Nest on ground.

Food: Lemmings (small arctic rodents) and Arctic hares.

Size: Twenty to 27 inches (51-69 centimeters) long. Females larger than males. Wingspread 50-60 inches (130-150 centimeters).

Life Span: Not known, perhaps 10 years or more.

Locomotion: Flight is strong, steady and direct but not rapid. Often sails for some distance.

Voice: Mostly silent, but its voice is described as a deep, hoarse "who-who." It has also been compared to the call of a raven.

What Can YOU Do?

There are many things we all can do to help preserve the values and beauties of the Arctic. The Arctic is a vast area, roughly three times the size of the lower 48 states. It is owned by seven countries: Canada, Greenland, Finland, Norway, Sweden, the Soviet Union and the United States. These countries all have their own ideas on how the Arctic should be developed for the good of their country. Oil, gas and other minerals are urgently needed. The weather is also a problem. The Arctic is frozen for six to eight months a year and some of the weather is severe. The time for action is very short. With all this in mind, here are some things that you can do to help guide the future of the Arctic.

What is the solution?

1. Contact the U.S. Ambassador to the United Nations to find out what the United States is doing to cooperate with the other countries in the Arctic. What is the United States doing to develop the natural resources wisely and to protect the wildlife there?

2. Encourage preservation of Alaskan wilderness. Proposals have been made to keep vast areas of Alaska untouched. This would prohibit development of roads, towns and mining. Write your members of Congress telling them that you support this idea.

3. The Alaskan pipe line brought big changes to the Arctic. We know that there are huge problems in getting oil out of the North Slope of Alaska. Learn how the construction of the pipe line has affected the tundra and the wildlife living there. Write to your Congressmen and express your concern about the future of this delicate area. Encourage them not to destroy the land and the wildlife.

Projects you can do

Plant a tundra
Find out what kinds of plants grow in the Arctic tundra. Then plant a tundra garden in your school yard or inside your classroom in a box. Remember that during the Arctic summer the sun never sets.

Build an igloo
If you live in snow country, build an igloo in your school yard. Use snow, water and a long knife to cut the blocks. (Styrofoam could be used instead of snow.) Then hold classes inside the igloo. Discuss how the Eskimos lived, the clothes they wore and how they depended on wildlife for their survival.

Visit Arctic wildlife at the zoo
Many Arctic animals can be found in the zoo. Almost every zoo has polar bears. Caribou, the Arctic fox, snowy owl and ptarmigan also are common in major zoos. Take a close look at the creatures that can survive in the world's toughest weather.

Write for more information
For Arctic information write: Arctic Institute of North America, 3458 Redpath Street, Montreal 109, Quebec, Canada; or 1619 New Hampshire Avenue, Washington, D.C. 20009; or University of Alaska, Institute of Marine Science, College, Alaska, 99701.

Arctic study questions

Find the answers to the questions about the Arctic and its wildlife. They will help you broaden your understanding of the region.

Arctic wildlife: Eight species are described in this book. How many more can you name?

Arctic plant life: There are about 1,790 different kinds of plants in the Arctic. Can you name 10?

North Pole: What is it like? Can a person walk on the North Pole?

Mineral wealth: Is the Arctic rich in minerals? What kinds and who owns them?

Other tundra: Where in North America, besides in the Arctic, can you find tundra?

American Arctic: How much of the Arctic territory does the United States own? What are Americans doing there?

Musk-ox/bison: White man's treatment of the Plains bison and the musk-ox is similar. How? What are the differences?

Snowmobiles: How has the snowmobile changed the life of the Eskimo?

White wildlife: Many of the Arctic creatures are white in winter. Why? How many of these animals can you name?

Cold Arctic: It is cold in both the Arctic and the Antarctic. Why? What is the coldest temperature ever recorded? Where?

Alaskan oil pipeline: How long is it? What special problems did it create for wildlife?

TEXT AND DESIGN: Market Communications, Inc.
Cliff Ganschow, chairman
H. Lee Schwanz, president
Glenn Helgeland, editorial director
Al Jacobs, art director
George Harrison, senior editor
Hal H. Harrison, Mada Harrison, Kit Harrison
and Valjean McLenighan, associate editors
Cheryl S. Bernard, Cynthia Swanson, Kathy
Sieja, Nanci Krajcir and Nancy Branson,
editorial assistants
Faith Williams, Robin Berens and Maureen Maguire,
production staff

PHOTOGRAPHERS: Gary Meszaros (Bruce Coleman, Inc.):
  Front Cover
George Harrison: Title Page, Page 32
Rollie Ostermick: Back Cover, Pages 8, 12, 34
Jen & Des Bartlett (Bruce Coleman, Inc.): Pages 26, 30
Bruce Coleman: Page 31
Sven Gillsater (Bruce Coleman, Inc.): Page 29
John M. Burnley (Bruce Coleman, Inc.): Page 28
Leonard Lee Rue III: Page 54
Leonard Lee Rue III (Bruce Coleman, Inc.): Pages 36-37
F. Erize (Bruce Coleman, Inc.): Pages 24, 40
Norman Owen Tomalin (Bruce Coleman, Inc.): Pages 38-39
Keith Gunnar (Bruce Coleman, Inc.): Page 11
Kenneth M. Giesen (Hal H. Harrison): Page 10
Gary R. Jones (Bruce Coleman, Inc.): Page 58
Eric Hosking (Bruce Coleman, Inc.): Page 59
Edgar T. Jones (Bruce Coleman, Inc.): Page 14
Rod Allin (Bruce Coleman, Inc.): Pages 50, 51, 56
A. J. Dignan (Bruce Coleman, Inc.): Page 60
Wolfgang Bayer (Bruce Coleman, Inc.): Pages 20, 44
Jerry L. Hout (Bruce Coleman, Inc.): Page 22
Erwin A. Bauer: Page 23
J. Simon (Bruce Coleman, Inc.): Pages 16-17
Robert L. Dunne (Bruce Coleman, Inc.): Page 42
A. R. McGregor (Bruce Coleman, Inc.): Page 45
Jane Burton (Bruce Coleman, Inc.): Page 46
Len Rue, Jr.: Page 48
Nicholas deVore III (Bruce Coleman, Inc.): Pages 52-53
K. W. Fink (Bruce Coleman, Inc.): Page 18

ART: Jay Blair: Pages 6-7